Saints *of the* Americas

REV. JUDE WINKLER, OFM Conv.

CONTENTS

Imprimi Potest: Michael Kolodziej, OFM Conv., Minister Provincial of St. Anthony of Padua Province (USA)
Nihil Obstat: Rev. Msgr. James M. Cafone, M.A., S.T.D., Censor Librorum
Imprimatur: ✠ **Most Rev. John J. Myers, J.C.D., D.D.**, Archbishop of Newark

The Nihil Obstat and Imprimatur are official declarations that a book or pamphlet is free of doctrinal or moral error. No implication is contained therein that those who have granted the Nihil Obstat and Imprimatur agree with the contents, opinions or statements expressed.

CPSIA   January 2014   10 9 8 7 6 5 4 3 2   A/P

© 2006 by CATHOLIC BOOK PUBLISHING CORP., Totowa, N.J.

Printed in Hong Kong   ISBN 978-0-89942-540-5

The Faith Arrives in America

IN 1492, Christopher Columbus sailed from Spain to find a new route to India. After months at sea, he landed on an island off the coast of the Americas, which he named San Salvador, the Island of Our Holy Savior. From his first days in the Americas, Columbus wanted to share our Faith.

One of the people who fought to protect the native peoples from brutal early explorers unlike Columbus was Roque Gonzalez de Santa Cruz (1576-1628). The son of a Spanish father and Paraguayan mother, Roque was born into a well-to-do family. Ordained at twenty-three years of age, he entered the Society of Jesus (Jesuits) in 1609, so that he could devote himself to missionary work.

He fought for the rights of the native peoples in the wilderness of Brazil and in surrounding countries, including Paraguay. He and his fellow Jesuits established some half a dozen large plantations, or colonies, where the natives could prosper and be safe from slave traders.

Alonso Rodriguez and Juan de Castillo, two younger Spanish Jesuits, joined Father Roque in his work in 1628. Later that year, as they continued to establish more colonies, their efforts were met with much hostility. Within two days, all three priests were savagely killed. Roque and his companions were canonized by Pope John Paul II in Paraguay in 1988.

Saint Juan Diego

(1474-1548)

GOD showed His love for the native peoples of America when He sent Mary to appear near Mexico City to one of the first Aztecs to convert to the Faith, Juan Diego. The site, Tepeyac, came to be known as Guadalupe.

On Saturday, December 9, 1531, Juan Diego was on his way to church when he heard many birds singing on a hilltop. He looked up and saw a bright light shining and heard a voice call to him.

Arriving atop the hill, he met a beautiful woman who told him that she was the ever-Virgin Holy Mary, Mother of the True God. She sent him to tell the Bishop to build a great church on that spot.

Mary continued to appear to Juan over the next days. Although he had told the Bishop about her message, the Bishop told him that he needed a sign.

Finally, Mary had Juan Diego pick roses on the hillside to fill his mantle (a strange request because roses normally do not bloom in the middle of the winter). When he emptied his mantle before the Bishop, they were all surprised that an image of Mary was imprinted on it. At last, the Bishop believed and had a great basilica built on that holy site.

Juan Diego was canonized in 2002. His feast day is December 9.

Saint Rose of Lima
(1586-1617)

and Saint Martin de Porres
(1579-1639)

THE city of Lima, Peru produced two great Saints early in the seventeenth century.

Rose of Lima was of Spanish descent. As a young girl, she wanted to give herself entirely to God. Her family strongly objected to the penances she performed, but she carried on with courage.

She set up a home for homeless children, the elderly, and the sick. Although she lived her Faith quietly, she nevertheless became famous throughout the city. When she died at only thirty-one, the whole city turned out for her funeral. In 1671, she was canonized by Pope Clement X.

The second great Saint of Lima was Martin de Porres. His father was Spanish and his mother was a mix of native and African blood. His father abandoned them when Martin was only eight, and he grew up in great poverty.

As a Dominican brother, he performed many works of charity. Martin took care of slaves, helped found an orphanage, and took care of the ill. Even during his lifetime he was famous for miracles performed through his intercession. He was declared a Saint by Pope John XXIII on May 6, 1962.

Saint Peter Claver

(1581-1654)

ABOUT this same time, St. Peter Claver, a young Jesuit, left Spain to work with slaves in the city of Cartagena, Colombia.

The slaves were brought from Africa in ships that were overcrowded and filled with disease. They were not thought of as being human and were treated like animals.

St. Peter would meet the ships as they arrived, and he would do his best to care for the slaves. He would give them food and medicine and would try to treat them with simple human dignity.

St. Peter would take care of not only the bodies of the slaves but also their souls. He shared our Faith with them. Many of their owners did not even care to have the Gospel preached to the slaves, because they did not consider them to be human beings. St. Peter refused to believe this, and he brought as many as 300,000 people into the Faith.

Whenever St. Peter would travel from the city, he chose to sleep in the slave quarters of the place where he was staying. His generosity toward the slaves embarrassed many of the rich people of his city, but when he died, even they had to acknowledge his holiness. He was canonized by Pope Leo XIII in 1888. His feast day is September 9.

Saint Isaac Jogues

(1607-1646)

WHILE the Spanish and Portuguese brought the Faith to Central and South America, it was the French who brought it to North America. Many missionaries came to share the Faith with the native peoples of New France (Canada and the northeastern United States).

Among the most famous of these is St. Isaac Jogues. He traveled to America in 1636 and worked among the Hurons. They were then at war with the Iroquois, and St. Isaac was captured by an Indian raiding party. He was held captive for thirteen months and tortured terribly. Finally, he found a way to escape and returned to France.

In captivity, he lost some of his fingers through torture. In those days, a priest could not celebrate Mass if something was wrong with his hands. The Pope himself gave St. Isaac permission to say Mass, because he had already suffered so much for the Faith.

He returned to Canada as soon as he could. In 1646, he set out to spread the Faith among the Iroquois who had recently made a peace treaty with the Hurons. He was captured by a Mohawk raiding party and put to death on October 18, just outside of what is presently Albany, New York. On June 29, 1930, he was canonized by Pope Pius XI.

Blessed Kateri Tekakwitha

(1656-1680)

ST. Isaac Jogues and the other French martyrs did not die in vain. There is a saying that the blood of the martyrs is the seed of the Church. The Faith spread quickly in North America.

One who converted was a young Mohawk woman named Kateri Tekakwitha. Her parents died from smallpox when she was only four. She was raised by her uncle who was the tribal chief. He hated the Christian missionaries but permitted them to live in his village because of a treaty the Mohawks had made with the French.

Though afraid of her uncle, she found the courage to convert. She was baptized on Easter Sunday when she was nineteen. She was treated horribly because of her conversion, but she used this suffering as a means to meditate upon God's love for her.

Eventually she traveled to a Christian village outside of Montreal. There she grew in love for the Lord, spending long hours in prayer and fasting. She vowed herself to virginity so that she could dedicate herself entirely to the Lord. She died when she was only twenty-four. Her face was scarred from childhood smallpox, but after her death her skin became as soft as a child's. In 1980, she was beatified by Pope John Paul II.

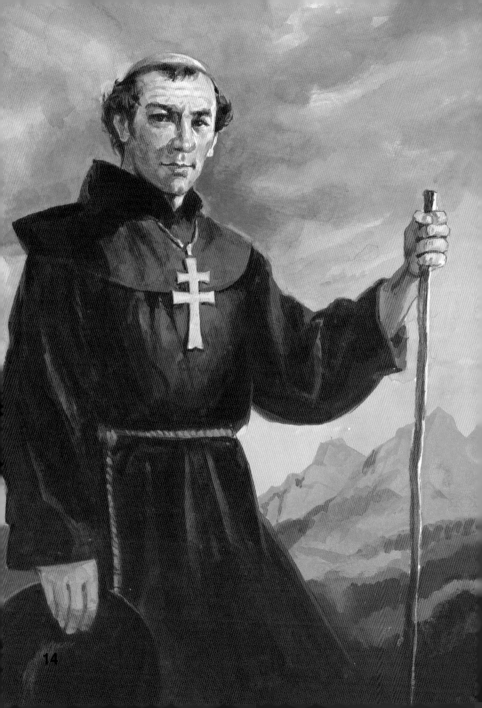

Blessed Junipero Serra

(1713-1784)

IN the late 1700s, the Church in Mexico decided to establish a series of missions in California.

Junipero Serra headed that missionary effort. Born in Spain, he joined the Franciscans when he was seventeen. He taught theology and was a famous preacher when he heard the call to the missions.

For years, Father Serra worked in the missions of Baja California (Mexico). In 1769, he founded San Diego, the first mission in California. The mission almost failed because of a lack of supplies, but he made a Novena to St. Joseph. On March 19, St. Joseph's feast day, a shipment of supplies arrived that permitted the mission to continue.

He founded twenty other missions and is said to have baptized some six thousand people. Father Serra protected the native peoples against civil and military authorities, although some things that he did to keep them safe may sound cruel today. He observed strict rules only to keep them from harm in a very dangerous age.

Father Serra often suffered not only hunger and illness but also danger from both the army and the natives. He always responded to these trials with prayer. He was beatified by Pope John Paul II in 1988.

Saint Elizabeth Ann Seton

(1774-1821)

ELIZABETH Seton was born in New York City. Her family was part of the high society of that city, and they belonged to the Episcopal Church.

When she was nineteen, Elizabeth married William Seton, a wealthy businessman. Deeply in love, they had five children. But among their hardships was William's failed business and ill health.

Before he died, they traveled to Italy in hope of finding a cure. While there, Elizabeth fell in love with the Catholic Faith. She was convinced that Jesus truly is present in the Eucharist. She believed that the Church started with the Apostles, and she had great love and devotion for our Lady.

Elizabeth converted to Catholicism in 1805 despite much opposition. She moved to Baltimore to raise her family. Just outside of the city, she opened the first free Catholic school.

By 1809 she had founded the first American congregation of religious sisters, the Sisters of Charity. They dedicated themselves to children's education and the care of orphans. Elizabeth continued to seek to follow the Lord's will, even in the face of losing many loved ones.

This first American-born Saint was canonized on September 14, 1975, by Pope Paul VI.

Saint Miguel Cordero

(1854-1910)

FRANCISCO Febres Cordero Muñoz was born in 1854 to a prominent family in Ecuador. He was not able to stand until age five. Then he saw a vision of the Blessed Mother and was cured.

He attended a school run by the Christian Brothers, and when he was of age, decided to join their congregation. He was accepted and became known as Brother Miguel.

Miguel's first assignment was in Quito, where he remained for thirty-two years. He was an outstanding teacher and wrote many books on education. The government of Ecuador adopted his texts for schools throughout the country. In 1892, Brother Miguel was elected to the national Academy of Letters.

Despite his fame in the field of education, Brother Miguel delighted in preparing the very young for their First Holy Communion. He also wrote manuals of piety, gave religious instruction, and conducted retreats.

Miguel died in 1910 in Spain and his body was returned to Ecuador with great public ceremony. His feast day is February 9.

Saint John Neumann

(1811-1860)

THE Catholic Church was very small when the United States gained its independence. Early in the 1800s, however, there was great growth as many immigrants from Catholic countries arrived.

Along with these immigrants were many missionaries. One of them was St. John Neumann. He came to America from Prague when he was twenty-five. His deep spiritual life led him to join the Redemptorists four years later. He traveled thousands of miles in New York State, Maryland, Virginia, and Ohio, establishing parishes wherever he went.

An effective priest, St. John was called to be a leader in the Church. First, he became a superior of the American Redemptorists; then, in 1852, he was made the Bishop of Philadelphia.

He spent his life visiting the parishes of his diocese, founding over eighty new churches and establishing Catholic grammar schools. He and St. Elizabeth Seton are largely responsible for the growth of Catholic education in the United States. In addition, he sponsored many colleges, hospitals, orphanages, and other ministries dedicated to the care of body and soul.

John Neumann was declared a Saint by Pope Paul VI in 1977. His feast day is January 5.

Saint Mariana of Quito

(1618-1645)

A TTRACTED to things religious from a very early age, Mariana dedicated herself completely to God.

She was born in Quito, Ecuador, in 1618. Her parents were of Spanish nobility, but she was orphaned as a child. Then, Mariana was raised with loving care by her sister.

At the age of twelve, she became a recluse in her sister's house, guided by her confessor, a Jesuit priest. Mariana never left that house for the rest of her life, except to go to church.

She ate very little, slept only three hours a night, and spent much time in prayer. Drawing close to God, Mariana had the gifts of prophecy and miracles.

In 1645, when Quito was ravaged by an earthquake and epidemic, she offered herself publicly as a victim for the sins of the people. The quake ended, and as the epidemic began to subside, Mariana fell ill and died on May 26, which became her feast day. Known as the "Lily of Quito," she was canonized by Pope Pius XII in 1950.

Saint Frances Xavier Cabrini

(1850-1917)

STILL another of the immigrant Saints was Mother Cabrini. Born in Italy, she joined the convent in 1877. She wanted to become a missionary to China, but Pope Leo XIII urged her to travel to America to serve the millions of immigrants who had arrived from Italy in recent years.

Her first project was to open an orphanage in New York City. When she arrived, the Archbishop informed her that her building was no longer available. He suggested that she return to Italy. Mother Cabrini refused to yield. She eventually found the needed building and opened the orphanage.

At her death, she had opened sixty-seven institutions for her fellow immigrants, and her congregation numbered about thirteen hundred. Mother Cabrini was terribly afraid of traveling by ship, yet she found courage to cross the ocean over thirty times in order to do her work. Despite the challenges she faced due to poor health, the opposition of city officials, and, at times, even of Church leaders, in all of her endeavors, she always abandoned herself to the love of the Sacred Heart of Jesus.

A sickly woman, she suffered from malaria, which eventually caused her death in Chicago. Her canonization by Pope Pius XII in 1946 was marked by the fact that she was the first American citizen so honored.

Blessed Marie Rose Durocher

(1811-1849)

BORN on October 6, 1811, at St. Antoine in Quebec, Canada, Eulalie Durocher was the youngest of ten children. After receiving her education from the Sisters of Notre Dame, she helped her brother, a parish priest.

In 1843, the Saint was invited by Bishop Bourget to found a new congregation of women that would be dedicated to Christian education. She thus founded the Sisters of the Holy Names of Jesus and Mary and took the religious name of Marie Rose.

Under her saintly and wise leadership, her community flourished despite a number of challenges. Among these were great poverty and misunderstandings that could not be avoided. In the face of so much, she stood firm in her concern for the poor.

The demands of her work were so great that, in only six short years after founding her community, she died on October 6, 1849, her thirty-eighth birthday.

She was declared Blessed by Pope John Paul II on May 23, 1982. Her feast day is celebrated on October 6.

Saint Katharine Drexel

(1858-1955)

KATHARINE Drexel was born in Philadelphia to a very wealthy family. From her mother, who cared for the poor, she learned a spirit of charity. She also learned from her a great love for the Blessed Sacrament.

While a young girl, Katharine shared her Faith by teaching Sunday school. She also sacrificed as she cared for her dying mother for three years.

Katherine always had a great interest in helping the Native American missions. She and her sisters built thirteen mission schools in the western United States. When she visited Pope Leo XIII, she asked him for more missionaries for this work. He asked her why she did not become a missionary.

She entered the novitiate in 1889 and professed her vows in the new congregation of the Sisters of the Blessed Sacrament for Indians and Colored People. She and her sisters built schools for Native and African Americans all throughout the country.

Many people fought her work, and one of her schools was burned, but she continued with great courage. She worked continuously until she was seventy-seven years old, when poor health forced her to retire. She spent the last twenty years of her life dedicated to prayer. Her canonization by Pope John Paul II took place on October 1, 2000.

Blessed Miguel Agustín Pro

(1891-1927)

THERE is nothing that says a Saint cannot have a good sense of humor, and Miguel Pro had such a good one that he could easily become the Patron Saint of practical jokes.

Born to a wealthy family in Guadalupe, Mexico, he was constantly playing jokes on his sisters and brothers. Miguel also was very talented at imitating voices and dressing up in disguises.

These traits were to prove very helpful in his work. He joined the Jesuits and was ordained a priest in 1925. At that time, the government of Mexico was persecuting the Church, and Miguel had to work in the underground in order to serve the faithful. Disguised, he would travel from place to place, celebrating Mass, listening to Confessions, and bringing Holy Communion. He also collected food and clothes for those being persecuted.

Once he saw the secret police guarding the place where he was supposed to celebrate Mass. Pretending he also was a policeman, he told them not to let any priests enter. He then entered the room and celebrated Mass for those gathered.

Finally, Miguel was captured and put to death before a firing squad. His last words were, "Long live Christ the King." He was beatified in 1988.

A Land of Saints

THE Americas continue to be fertile ground for the growth of Saints. The martyrs' blood, shed from the days of Columbus, continues to be the seed of the Faith.

Many heroes of the Faith have died in recent times. In Central America, Archbishop Romero died for defending the poor. In South America, Franciscan Friars Miguel and Zbigniew were killed by Communist rebels for feeding the poor.

The late twentieth century bore witness to heroes of charity dedicated to lives of service. Among these were Dorothy Day of the Catholic Worker movement and Terence Cardinal Cooke of New York City. The call today is still the same as it was in the days of Jesus, "Come, follow Me."